Fractions

Making Fair Shares

by Michele Koomen

Consultant:
Deborah S. Ermoian
Mathematics Faculty
Phoenix College
Phoenix, Arizona

Bridgestone Books
an imprint of Capstone Press
Mankato, Minnesota

Bridgestone Books are published by Capstone Press
151 Good Counsel Drive, P.O. Box 669, Mankato, Minnesota 56002
http://www.capstone-press.com

Library of Congress Cataloging-in-Publication Data
Koomen, Michele.
    Fractions: making fair shares/by Michele Koomen.
    p. cm.—(Exploring math)
    Includes bibliographical references and index.
    ISBN 0-7368-0817-5
    1. Fractions—Juvenile literature. [1. Fractions.] I. Title. II. Series.
QA117 .K66 2001
513.2′6—dc21   00-010566

Summary: Simple text, photographs, and illustrations introduce fractions by showing
    children dividing a candy bar, a pizza, a rope of licorice, and a pie into fair shares.

Editorial Credits
Tom Adamson, editor; Lois Wallentine, product planning editor; Linda Clavel, designer;
    Katy Kudela, photo researcher

Photo Credits
Capstone Press/CG Book Printers, 4
Kimberly Danger, 6, 8, 10, 12 (all), 14, 16 (all), 17, 18, 20
PhotoDisc, Inc., cover

1 2 3 4 5 6 06 05 04 03 02 01

Table of Contents

What Is a Fraction?

We sometimes need to divide a whole object into equal pieces. We describe these pieces by using numbers called fractions.

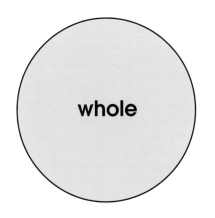

whole

fraction

Equal Shares

These two kids have one whole candy bar. They each would like to have an equal piece of the candy bar. They will need to break the bar to share it.

1 fair share $\longrightarrow$ $\dfrac{1}{2}$

2 pieces $\longrightarrow$

Halves

The kids break the candy bar in the middle. Each kid then has a fair share. A fair share means that they each have the same amount. Each kid has one-half of the candy bar. One-half ($\frac{1}{2}$) is a fraction. Two halves make one whole.

Fourths

One whole pizza is too much for
one kid to eat. It is not too much
for four kids. They can cut the pizza
into four equal pieces to share it.

1 fair share ⟶ $\dfrac{1}{4}$

4 pieces ⟶

Dividing into Fourths

First the kids cut the pizza in half. They then cut each half in half again. Now there are four pieces. One-fourth of the pizza is a fair share for each kid. One-fourth ($\frac{1}{4}$) is a fraction. Each fourth is the same size.

Thirds

This whole rope of licorice is too much for one kid to eat. The rope will be just right for three kids to share. The licorice needs to be cut into three pieces.

Dividing into Thirds

The kids fold the licorice into three equal pieces. They then cut the licorice where it folds. Now there are three pieces of licorice.

1 fair share ⟶ $\dfrac{1}{3}$

3 pieces

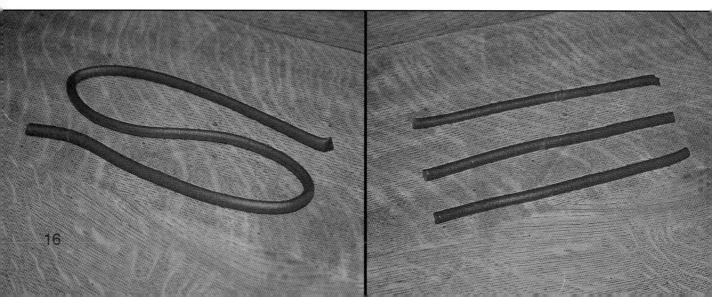

One-third of the licorice is a fair share for each kid. One-third ($\frac{1}{3}$) is a fraction.

Sixths

One whole pecan pie is too much for one kid to eat. The pie is not too much for six kids. They need to cut the pie into six equal pieces.

1 fair share → $\dfrac{1}{6}$

6 pieces → $\dfrac{1}{6}$

Dividing into Sixths

The kids cut the pie into six equal pieces. Each piece is one-sixth of the pie. One-sixth of the pie is a fair share for each kid. One-sixth ($\frac{1}{6}$) is a fraction.

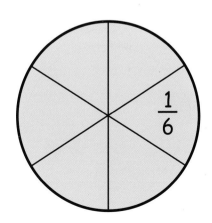

Hands On: Make Paper Fractions

What You Need

4 pieces of construction paper
Scissors
Marker or pen

What You Do

1. Fold one piece of paper in half lengthwise. Crease it well.

2. Cut the paper on the creased line. These two pieces of paper are halves. Write $\frac{1}{2}$ on each piece.

3. Fold another piece of paper in half lengthwise. Fold it in half again. Crease it well.

4. Open the piece of paper. Cut it on the creased lines. You will have four pieces of paper that are the same size. These are fourths. Write $\frac{1}{4}$ on each piece.

5. Fold another piece of paper into three equal pieces. Cut along the folded lines. You will have three pieces of paper. These are thirds. Write $\frac{1}{3}$ on each piece.

6. Compare the sizes of each fraction of paper to the whole piece of paper. Which is bigger, one-third or one-half? How many fourths equal one-half?

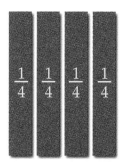

Words to Know

crease (KREESS)—to make a fold in something

equal (EE-kwuhl)—the same as something else; you can break a candy bar into two equal halves.

fair (FAYR)—reasonable and just; it is fair to give the same amount to everyone.

fraction (FRAK-shuhn)—a number that tells us about the pieces of a whole

whole (HOHL)—all the parts of something; two halves make one whole.

Read More

Adler, David A. *Fraction Fun.* New York: Holiday House, 1996.

King, Andrew. *Making Fractions.* Math for Fun. Brookfield, Conn.: Copper Beech Books, 1998.

Pallotta, Jerry. *The Hershey's Milk Chocolate Bar Fractions Book.* New York: Cartwheel Books, 1999.

Scieszka, Jon, and Lane Smith. *Math Curse.* New York: Viking, 1995.

Internet Sites

Ask Dr. Math
http://mathforum.com/dr.math
Aunty Math
http://www.dcmrats.org/auntymath.html
Figure This! Math Challenges for Families
http://www.figurethis.org

Index